On the incarnation. A sermon, preached in the parish church of St. Mary Newington, in Surrey, Dec. 25, 1785. By ... Samuel Horsley, ...

Samuel Horsley

Eighteenth Century
Collections Online
Print Editions

Gale ECCO Print Editions

Relive history with *Eighteenth Century Collections Online*, now available in print for the independent historian and collector. This series includes the most significant English-language and foreign-language works printed in Great Britain during the eighteenth century, and is organized in seven different subject areas including literature and language; medicine, science, and technology; and religion and philosophy. The collection also includes thousands of important works from the Americas.

The eighteenth century has been called "The Age of Enlightenment." It was a period of rapid advance in print culture and publishing, in world exploration, and in the rapid growth of science and technology – all of which had a profound impact on the political and cultural landscape. At the end of the century the American Revolution, French Revolution and Industrial Revolution, perhaps three of the most significant events in modern history, set in motion developments that eventually dominated world political, economic, and social life.

In a groundbreaking effort, Gale initiated a revolution of its own: digitization of epic proportions to preserve these invaluable works in the largest online archive of its kind. Contributions from major world libraries constitute over 175,000 original printed works. Scanned images of the actual pages, rather than transcriptions, recreate the works *as they first appeared.*

Now for the first time, these high-quality digital scans of original works are available via print-on-demand, making them readily accessible to libraries, students, independent scholars, and readers of all ages.

For our initial release we have created seven robust collections to form one the world's most comprehensive catalogs of 18th century works.

Initial Gale ECCO Print Editions collections include:

History and Geography
Rich in titles on English life and social history, this collection spans the world as it was known to eighteenth-century historians and explorers. Titles include a wealth of travel accounts and diaries, histories of nations from throughout the world, and maps and charts of a world that was still being discovered. Students of the War of American Independence will find fascinating accounts from the British side of conflict.

Social Science

Delve into what it was like to live during the eighteenth century by reading the first-hand accounts of everyday people, including city dwellers and farmers, businessmen and bankers, artisans and merchants, artists and their patrons, politicians and their constituents. Original texts make the American, French, and Industrial revolutions vividly contemporary.

Medicine, Science and Technology

Medical theory and practice of the 1700s developed rapidly, as is evidenced by the extensive collection, which includes descriptions of diseases, their conditions, and treatments. Books on science and technology, agriculture, military technology, natural philosophy, even cookbooks, are all contained here.

Literature and Language

Western literary study flows out of eighteenth-century works by Alexander Pope, Daniel Defoe, Henry Fielding, Frances Burney, Denis Diderot, Johann Gottfried Herder, Johann Wolfgang von Goethe, and others. Experience the birth of the modern novel, or compare the development of language using dictionaries and grammar discourses.

Religion and Philosophy

The Age of Enlightenment profoundly enriched religious and philosophical understanding and continues to influence present-day thinking. Works collected here include masterpieces by David Hume, Immanuel Kant, and Jean-Jacques Rousseau, as well as religious sermons and moral debates on the issues of the day, such as the slave trade. The Age of Reason saw conflict between Protestantism and Catholicism transformed into one between faith and logic -- a debate that continues in the twenty-first century.

Law and Reference

This collection reveals the history of English common law and Empire law in a vastly changing world of British expansion. Dominating the legal field is the *Commentaries of the Law of England* by Sir William Blackstone, which first appeared in 1765. Reference works such as almanacs and catalogues continue to educate us by revealing the day-to-day workings of society.

Fine Arts

The eighteenth-century fascination with Greek and Roman antiquity followed the systematic excavation of the ruins at Pompeii and Herculaneum in southern Italy; and after 1750 a neoclassical style dominated all artistic fields. The titles here trace developments in mostly English-language works on painting, sculpture, architecture, music, theater, and other disciplines. Instructional works on musical instruments, catalogs of art objects, comic operas, and more are also included.

The BiblioLife Network

This project was made possible in part by the BiblioLife Network (BLN), a project aimed at addressing some of the huge challenges facing book preservationists around the world. The BLN includes libraries, library networks, archives, subject matter experts, online communities and library service providers. We believe every book ever published should be available as a high-quality print reproduction; printed on-demand anywhere in the world. This insures the ongoing accessibility of the content and helps generate sustainable revenue for the libraries and organizations that work to preserve these important materials.

The following book is in the "public domain" and represents an authentic reproduction of the text as printed by the original publisher. While we have attempted to accurately maintain the integrity of the original work, there are sometimes problems with the original work or the micro-film from which the books were digitized. This can result in minor errors in reproduction. Possible imperfections include missing and blurred pages, poor pictures, markings and other reproduction issues beyond our control. Because this work is culturally important, we have made it available as part of our commitment to protecting, preserving, and promoting the world's literature.

GUIDE TO FOLD-OUTS MAPS and OVERSIZED IMAGES

The book you are reading was digitized from microfilm captured over the past thirty to forty years. Years after the creation of the original microfilm, the book was converted to digital files and made available in an online database.

In an online database, page images do not need to conform to the size restrictions found in a printed book. When converting these images back into a printed bound book, the page sizes are standardized in ways that maintain the detail of the original. For large images, such as fold-out maps, the original page image is split into two or more pages

Guidelines used to determine how to split the page image follows:

• Some images are split vertically; large images require vertical and horizontal splits.
• For horizontal splits, the content is split left to right.
• For vertical splits, the content is split from top to bottom.
• For both vertical and horizontal splits, the image is processed from top left to bottom right.

ON THE INCARNATION.

A

SERMON,

BY

The Rev. SAMUEL HORSLEY, LL. D. F. R. S.

ON THE INCARNATION.

A

SERMON,

Preached in the Parish Church of St. Mary Newington,
in Surrey, Dec. 25, 1785.

BY

The Rev. SAMUEL HORSLEY, LL. D. F. R. S.

ARCHDEACON of St. ALBAN's, and CHAPLAIN to the RIGHT REV.
FATHER IN GOD, ROBERT, LORD BISHOP OF LONDON.

LONDON.
PRINTED FOR JAMES ROBSON, BOOKSELLER,
IN NEW BOND STREET.

MDCCLXXXII

LUKE I 28.

—— HAIL THOU THAT ART HIGHLY FAVOURED, THE LORD IS WITH
THEE. BLESSED ART THOU AMONG WOMEN.

THAT fhe, who in thefe terms was faluted by an angel,
fhould in after-ages become an object of fuperftitious
adoration, is a thing far lefs to be wondered, than that men pro-
feffing to build their whole hopes of immortality on the promifes delivered in the facred books, and clofely interwoven
with the hiftory of our Saviour's Life, fhould queftion the
truth of the meffage which the angel brought. Some nine
years fince the Chriftian Church was no lefs aftonifhed than
offended, by an extravagant attempt [a] to heighten, as it was
pretended, the importance of the Chriftian Revelation, by
overturning one of thofe firft principles, of natural religion,

[a] Difquifitions relating to Matter and Spirit, &c London. 1777

A 2

which

which had for ages been confidered as the bafis, upon which the whole fuperftructure of Revelation ftands. The notion of an immaterial principle in man, which, without an immediate ex-ertion of the divine power to the exprefs purpofe of its deftruc-tion, muft neceffarily furvive the diffolution of the body; the notion of an immortal foul, was condemned and exploded as an invention of heathen philofophy. Death was reprefented as an utter extinction of the whole man, and the evangelical doc-trine of a refurrection of the body, in an improved ftate, to re-ceive again its immortal inhabitant, was heightened into the myftery of a re-production of the annihilated perfon. How a perfon once annihilated could be re-produced, fo as to be the fame perfon which had formerly exifted, when no principle of famenefs, nothing neceffarily permanent, was fuppofed to enter the original compofition; how the prefent perfon could be interefted in the future perfon's fortunes; why *I* fhould be at all concerned for the happinefs or mifery of the man, who fome ages hence fhall be raifed from my afhes; when the fu-ture man could be no otherwife the fame with me, than as he was arbitrarily to be called the fame, becaufe his body was to be compofed of the fame matter which now compofes mine : thefe difficulties were but ill explained. It was thought a fufficient recommendation of the fyftem with all its difficulties, that the promife of a refurrection of the body feemed to acquire a new importance from it (but the truth is, that it would lofe its whole importance, if this fyftem could be eftablifhed, fince it would become a mere prediction concerning a future race of men, and would be no promife to any men now exifting), and the notion of the foul's natural immortality was deemed an

unfeemly

unseemly appendage of a Christian's belief, for this singular reason, that it had been entertained by wise and virtuous Heathens, who had received no light from the Christian, nor, as it was supposed, from any earlier Revelation.

It might have been expected, that this anxiety to extinguish every ray of hope, which beams not from the glorious promises of the Gospel, would have been accompanied with the most entire submission of the understanding to the letter of the written word; the most anxious sollicitude for the credit of the sacred writers; the warmest zeal to maintain every circumstance in the history of our Saviour's life, which might add authority to his precepts, and weight to his promises, by heightening the dignity of his person. But so inconsistent with itself is human folly; that they who at one time seemed to think it a preliminary, to be required of every one who would come to a right belief of the Gospel, that he should unlearn and unbelieve what Philosophy had been thought to have in common with the Gospel, as if reason and revelation could in nothing agree; upon other occasions discover an aversion to the belief of any thing, which at all puts our reason to a stand: and in order to wage war with mystery with the more advantage, they scruple not to deny, that that Spirit which enlightened the first preachers in the delivery of their oral instruction, and rendered them infallible teachers of the age in which they lived, directed them in the composition of those writings, which they left for the edification of succeeding ages [a]. They pretend

[a] "I have frequently declared myself not to be a believer in the inspiration of the Evangelists and Apostles as writers." Dr. Priestley's Letters to Dr. H. Part I. p. 132.

to

to have made difcoveries of inconclufive reafoning in the Epiftles [a]; of doubtfull facts in the Gofpels; and, appealing from
the teftimony of the Apoftles to their own judgements, they
have not fcrupled to declare their opinion, that the *Miraculous
Conception of our Lord* is a fubject, " with refpect to which any
" perfon is at full liberty to think, as the evidence fhall appear
" to him, without any impeachment of his faith or character
" as a Chriftian [b]. And left a fimple avowal of this extraordi-
nary opinion fhould not be fufficiently offenfive, it is accompanied with certain obfcure infinuations [c], the referved mean-
ing of which we are little anxious to divine, which feem in-
tended to prepare the world not to be furprized, if fomething
ftill more extravagant, if more extravagant may be, fhould in a
little be declared.

We are affembled this day to commemorate our Lord's Nativity.
It is not as the Birth-day of a Prophet that this day is fanctified;
but as the Anniverfary of that great event, which had been announced by the whole fucceffion of Prophets from the beginning
of the world, and in which the predictions concerning the manner
of the Meffiah's advent received their compleat and literal ac-
complifhment. In the predictions, as well as in the corefpond-
ing event, the circumftance of the Miraculous Conception makes
fo principal a part, that we fhall not eafily find fubjects of me-
ditation more fuited either to the feafon, or to the times,
than thefe two points; the importance of this doctrine, as an

[a] Hiftory of Corruption, vol II p. 370.
[b] Letter to Dr. H part I p. 132
[c] Letter to Dr H part I. p 54

2

article

article of the Chriftian faith, and the fufficiency of the evidence by which the fact is fupported.

Firft for the importance of the doctrine, as an article of the Chriftian faith; it is evidently the foundation of the whole diftinction between the character of Chrift, in the condition of a man, and that of any other Prophet. Had the conception of Jefus been in the natural way; had he been the fruit of Mary's marriage with her hufband; his intercourfe with the Deity could have been of no other kind, than the nature of any other man might have equally admitted: an intercourfe of no higher kind than the Prophets enjoyed, when their minds were enlightened by the extraordinary influence of the Holy Spirit. The information conveyed to Jefus might have been clearer and more extenfive, than any imparted to any former Prophet; but the manner and the means of communication muft have been the fame. The Holy Scriptures fpeak a very different language. They tell us, that the " fame God who fpake in " times paft to the Fathers by the Prophets, hath in thefe latter " days fpoken unto us by his Son [a];" evidently eftablifhing a diftinction of Chriftianity from preceding Revelations upon a diftinction between the two characters of a Prophet of God, and of God's Son. Mofes, the great Lawgiver of the Jews, is defcribed in the book of DEUTERONOMY as fuperior to all fucceeding Prophets for the intimacy of his intercourfe with God, for the variety of his miracles, and for the authority with which he was invefted. " There arofe not a Prophet in Ifrael like unto " Mofes, whom Jehovah knew face to face: in all the figns and wonders which Jehovah fent him to do in the land

[a] Heb. I. 1, 2.

" of

" of Egypt to Pharaoh and all his fervants, and to all his land; " and in all that mighty hand, and in all the great terror, " which Mofes fhewed in the fight of all Ifrael [a]." Yet this great Prophet, raifed up to be the leader and the legiflator of God's people; this greateft of the Prophets, with whom Jehovah converfed face to face, as a man talketh with his friend; bore, we are told, to Jefus, the humble relation of a fervant to a fon [b]. And left the fuperiority on the fide of the Son fhould be deemed a meer fuperiority of the office to which he was appointed, we are told, that the Son is " higher than the angels," being the " effulgence of God's glory, the exprefs image of his " perfon [c]," the God " whofe throne is for ever and ever, " the fcepter of whofe kingdom is a fcepter of righteoufnefs [d]:" and this high dignity of the Son is alleged as a motive for a religious obedience to his commands, and for reliance on his promifes. It is this indeed which gives fuch authority to his precepts, and fuch certainty to his whole doctrine, as render faith in him the firft duty of religion. Had Chrift been a meer Prophet, to believe in Chrift had been the fame thing as to believe in John the Baptift. The meffages indeed, announced on the part of God by Chrift, and by John the Baptift, might have been different; and the importance of the different meffages, unequal, but the principle of belief in either muft have been the fame.

Hence it appears, that the intercourfe which Chrift, as a man, held with God, was different in kind from that which the

[a] Deut xxxiv. 10—12.   [b] Heb. iii. 5 6.

[c] Heb i 3—6   [d] Heb. i. 8.

greateft

greateſt of the Prophets ever had enjoyed; and yet how it ſhould differ, otherwiſe than in the degree of frequency and intimacy, it will not be very eaſy to explain, unleſs we adhere to the faith tranſmitted to us from the primitive ages, and believe that the Eternal Word, who was in the beginning with God, and was God, ſo joined to himſelf the holy thing which was formed in Mary's womb, that the two natures, from the commencement of the Virgin's conception, made one perſon. Between God and any living being, having a diſtinct perſonality of his own ſeparate from the Godhead, no other communion could obtain; than what ſhould conſiſt in the action of the Divine Spirit upon the faculties of the ſeparate perſon. This communion with God the Prophets enjoyed. But Jeſus, according to the primitive doctrine, was ſo united to the ever-living word, that the very exiſtence of the man conſiſted in this union [a]. We ſhall

[a] So Theodoret in the fourth of the ſeven dialogues about the Trinity, publiſhed under the name of Athanaſius. The perſons in this dialogue are an Orthodox Believer and an Apollinarian. The Apollinarian aſks, Ουκ εϛιν ϰν Ιησϰς ανθρωπος; the Believer replies, ανευ τϰ Λογϰ ϰτε ανθρωπον αυτον οιδα ὑποϛανϊα, την γαρ ὑπαρξιν αυτϰ εν τη ἑνωσει τϰ Λογϰ γνωριζω. To the ſame purpoſe Joannnes Damaſcenus, ——— ϰ γαρ ϖρουϖοϛασϊ καθ' ἑαυϊην σαρκι ἡνωθη ὁ θειος Λογος, αλλ' ενοικησας τη γαϛρι της ἁγιας ϖαρθενϰ απεριγραπϊως, εν τη ἑαυϊϰ ὑποϛασει εκ των ἁγιων της αειπαρθενϰ ἁιμαϊων, σαρκα εψυχωμενην ψυχη λογικη τε και νοερα ὑπεϛησαϊο, απαρχην ϖροσλαϐομεν⅁ τϰ ανθρωπειϰ φυραμαϊ⅁, ΑΥΤΟΣ ῾Ο ΛΟΓΟΣ ΓΕΝΟΜΕΝΟΣ ΤΗ ΣΑΡΚΙ ῾ΥΠΟΣΤΑΣΙΣ. De Fide Orthodoxâ, lib. 3 cap. II. and again, cap. VII. εσαρκωϊαι τοινυν ——————— ὡϛε αὑϊην χρημαϊισαι τη σαρκι ὑποϛασιν ἡ τϰ θεϰ Λογϰ ὑποϛασις. So alſo Gregory Nazianzen, ἐι τις διαπεπλαϗῃ τον ανθρωπον, ειθ' ὑποδεδυκεναι λεγοι θεον, καϊακριϊος. ——————— ειτις ὡς εν ϖροφηϊη λεγοι καϊα χαριν ενηργηκεναι, αλλα μη καϊ' ϰσιαν συνηφθαι τε ϰαι συναπϊϗῃ, ειη κενος της κειρϊον⅁ ενεργειας, μαλλον δε ϖληρης της εναντιας. Epiſt. ad Cledon. I.

B

not

not indeed find this propofition, that the exiftence of Mary's Son confifted from the firft, and ever fhall confift, in his union with the Word; we fhall not find this propofition in thefe terms in Scripture. Would to God the neceffity never had arifen of ftating the difcoveries of Revelation in metaphyfical propofitions. The infpired writers delivered their fublimeft doctrines in popular language, and abftained as much as poffible from a philofophical phrafeology. By the perpetual cavils of gainfayers, and the difficulties which they have raifed; later teachers, in the affertion of the fame doctrines, have been reduced to the unpleafing neceffity of availing themfelves of the greater precifion of a lefs familiar language.

But if we find not the fame propofition in the fame words in Scripture, we find in Scripture what amounts to a clear proof of the propofition. We find the characteriftic properties of both natures, the Human and the Divine, afcribed to the fame per-fon. We read of Jefus, that he fuffered from hunger and from fatigue: That he wept for grief, and was diftreffed with fear: That he was obnoxious to all the evils of humanity, except the propenfity to fin. We read of the fame Jefus, that he had " Glory with the Father before the world hegan" [a]; that " all " things were created by him [b], both in heaven and in earth, " vifible and invifible; whether they be thrones, or dominions, " or principalities, or powers; all things were created by him " and for him" [c]; and " he upholdeth all things by the word " of his power [d]." And that we may in fome fort underftand,

[a] John xvii 5   [b] John i 3
[c] Coloff i 16   [d] Heb. i 3

how

how infirmity and perfection fhould thus meet in the fame perfon; we are told by St. John, that the " Word was made " Flefh."

It was clearly therefore the doctrine of Holy Writ; and nothing elfe, which the Fathers afferted in terms borrowed from the fchools of Philofophy, when they affirmed that the very principle of perfonality and individual exiftence in Mary's Soul was union with the uncreated Word [a]. A doctrine in which a Miraculous Conception would have been implied, had the thing not been recorded; fince a man, conceived in the ordinary way, would have derived the principles of his exiftence from the meer phyfical powers of generation. Union with the Divine Nature could not have been the principle of an exiftence phyfically derived from Adam; and that intimate union of God and man in the Redeemer's perfon, which the Scriptures fo clearly affert, had been a phyfical impoffibility.

But we need not go fo high, as to the Divine Nature of our Lord, to evince the neceffity of his Miraculous Conception. It was neceffary to the fcheme of Redemption by the Redeemer's

[a] Ὁ ων Θεος Λογο, σαρκωθεις, ετε την εν τη ψιλη θεωρια ναλανοεμενην φυσιν ανελαβεν (ε γαρ σαρκωσις τελο, αλλ' απαλη και πλασμα σαρκωσεως) ετε την εν τω ειδει θεωρεμενην (ε γαρ πασας τας υποςασεις ανελαβεν) αλλα την εν αλομω, την αυτην ὁσαν τη εν τω ειδει (απαρχην γαρ ανελαβε τα ἡμετερε φυραμαῑℂ⟩) ε καθ' ἑαυτην υποςα-σαν και ατομον χρηματισασαν προτερον, και ετι, υπ' αυτα προσληφθεισαν, αλλ' εν τη αυτε υποςασει ὑπαρξασαν· αυτη γαρ ἡ ὑποςασις τε Θεε Λογε εγενετο τη σαρκ, ὑποςασις. Joann Damafcen. De Fide Orthodoxâ, lib. 3. cap XI.

offering

offering of himſelf as an expiatory Sacrifice; that the manner of
his Conception ſhould be ſuch, that he ſhould in no degree
partake of the natural pollution of the fallen race, whoſe guilt
he came to atone, nor be included in the general condemnation
of Adam's progeny. In what the ſtain of original ſin may
conſiſt, and in what manner it may be propagated, it is not to
my preſent purpoſe to enquire. It is ſufficient that Adam's crime,
by the appointment of Providence, involved his whole poſte-
rity in puniſhment. " In Adam," ſays the Apoſtle, " all die [a]."
And for many lives thus forfeited, a ſingle life, itſelf a forfeit,
had been no ranſom. Nor by the Divine ſentence only, inflict-
ing death on the progeny, for the offence of the progenitor;
but by the proper guilt of his own ſins, every one ſprung by
natural deſcent from the loins of Adam is a debtor to Divine
Juſtice, and incapable of becoming a mediator for his brethren.
" In many things," ſays St. James, " we offend all [b]. If
" we ſay that we have no ſin, we deceive ourſelves," ſaith
St. John, " and the truth is not in us. And if any man ſin,
" we have an advocate with the Father, Jeſus Chriſt the
" righteous, and he is the propitiation for our ſins [c]." Even
we Chriſtians all offend, without exception even of the firſt
and beſt Chriſtians, the Apoſtles. But St. John clearly ſepa-
rates the righteous advocate from the maſs of thoſe offenders.
That any Chriſtian is enabled, by the aſſiſtance of God's Spirit, to attain to that degree of purity which may entitle him to
the future benefits of the Redemption, is itſelf a preſent benefit

[a] 1 Cor xv. 22.   [b] James iii. 2.
[c] 1 John, 1. 8. and ii. 1.

of

of the propitiation which hath been made for us : and he, who under the affault of every temptation maintained that unfullied innocence, which gives merit and efficacy to his Sacrifice and Interceffion, could not be of the number of thofe, whofe offences called for an expiation, and whofe frailties needed a Divine af-fiftance, to raife them effectually from dead works to ferve the Living God. In brief, the condemnation and the iniquity of Adam's progeny were univerfal. To reverfe the univerfal fen-tence, and to purge the univerfal corruption, a Redeemer was to be found pure of every ftain of inbred and contracted guilt. And fince every perfon produced in the natural way could not but be of the contaminated race ; the purity, requifite to the ef-ficacy of the Redeemer's Atonement, made it neceffary, that the manner of his Conception fhould be fupernatural.

Thus you fee the neceffary connection of the Miraculous Con-ception with the other articles of the Chriftian faith. The incar-nation of the Divine Word, fo roundly afferted by St. John, and fo clearly implied in innumerable paffages of Holy Writ, in any other way had been impoffible ; and the Redeemer's Atonement, inadequate and ineffectual. Infomuch that, had the extraordi-nary manner of our Lord's generation made no part of the evangelical narrative, the opinion might have been defended, as a thing clearly implied in the evangelical doctrine.

On the other hand, it were not difficult to fhew, that the Miraculous Conception, once admitted, naturally brings up after it the great doctrines of the Atonement and the Incarnation.

The

The Miraculous Conception of our Lord, evidently implies fome higher purpofe of his coming, than the mere bufinefs of a teacher. The bufinefs of a teacher might have been performed by a mere man, enlightened by the prophetic fpirit. For whatever inftruction men have the capacity to receive, a man might have been made the inftrument to convey. Had teaching therefore been the fole purpofe of our Saviour's coming, a mere man might have done the whole bufinefs; and the fupernatural conception had been an unneceffary miracle. He therefore, who came in this miraculous way, came upon fome higher bufinefs, to which a mere man was unequal. He came to be made a fin-offering for us, "that we might be made the righte-" oufnefs of God in him [a]."

So clofe therefore is the connection of this extraordinary fact with the cardinal doctrines of the Gofpel, that it may be juftly deemed a neceffary branch of the fcheme of Redemption: and in no other light was it confidered by St. Paul, who mentions it among the characteriftics of the Redeemer, that he fhould be " made of a woman [b]." In this fhort fentence St. Paul bears a remarkable teftimony to the truth of the evangelical hiftory in this circumftance. And *you*, my brethren, have not fo learned Chrift, but that you will prefer the teftimony of St. Paul to the rafh judgement of thofe, who have

[a] 2 Cor. v. 21.

[b] Gal iv 4 " There is no reference to the Miraculous Conception either " in the Book of Acts, or *in any of the Epiftles* " Dr Prieftley's Letters to Dr. H. P. 53.

dared

dared to tax this " chofen veffel" of the Lord with error and in-accuracy.

The opinion of thefe men is indeed the lefs to be regarded ; for the want of infight, which they difcover, into the real inte-refts and proper connections of their own fyftem. It is by no means fufficient for their purpofe, that they infift not on the belief of the Miraculous Conception. They muft infift upon the difbelief of it ; if they expect to make difcerning men pro-felytes to their Socinian doctrine. They muft difprove it ; be-fore they can reduce the Gofpel to what their fcheme of inter-pretation makes it ; a mere religion of nature, a fyftem of the beft practical Deifm, enforced by the fanction of high re-wards, and formidable punifhments, in a future life ; which are yet no rewards and no punifhments, but fimply the enjoyments and the fufferings of a new race of men to be made out of old materials, and therefore conftitute no fanction, when the principles of the materialift are incorporated with thofe of the Socinian in the finifhed creed of the modern Unitarian.

Having feen the importance of the doctrine of the Miracu-lous Conception, as an article of our faith ; let us in the next place confider the fufficiency of the evidence, by which the fact is fupported.

We have for it the exprefs teftimony of two out of the four Evangelifts : of St. Matthew, whofe Gofpel was publifhed

in:

in Judæa within a few years after our Lord's Afcenfion; and of St. Luke, whofe narrative was compofed, as may be collected from the author's fhort preface, to prevent the mifchief that was to be apprehended from fome pretended hiftories of our Saviour's life, in which the truth was probably blended with many legendary tales. It is very remarkable, that the fact of the Miraculous Conception fhould be found in the firft of the four Gofpels; written at a time when many of the near relations of the Holy Family muft have been living, by whom the ftory, had it been falfe, had been eafily confuted: that it fhould be found again in St. Luke's Gofpel; written for the peculiar ufe of the converted Gentiles, and for the exprefs purpofe of furnifhing a fummary of authentic facts, and of fuppreffing fpurious narrations. Was it not ordered by fome peculiar providence of God, that the two great branches of the primitive church; the Hebrew congregations, for which St. Matthew wrote, and the Greek congregations for which St. Luke wrote; fhould find an exprefs record of the Miraculous Conception each in its proper Gofpel? Or if we confider the teftimony of the writers, fimply as hiftorians of the times in which they lived, without regard to their infpiration, which is not admitted by the adverfary; were not Matthew and Luke, Matthew, one of the twelve Apoftles of our Lord, and Luke, the companion of St. Paul, competent to examine the evidence of the facts, which they have recorded? Is it likely that they have recorded facts, upon the credit of a vague report, without examination? And was it referved for the Unitarians of the eighteenth century to detect their errors? St. Luke thought

himfelf

himſelf particularly well qualified for the work, in which he engaged, by his exact knowledge of the ſtory, which he undertook to write, in all its circumſtances from the very beginning. It is ſaid indeed by a writer of the very firſt antiquity, and high in credit, that his Goſpel was compoſed from St. Paul's ſermons. " Luke, the attendant of St. Paul," ſays Irenæus, " put " into his book the Goſpel preached by that Apoſtle." This being premiſed, attend I beſeech you, to the account which St. Luke gives of his own undertaking. " It ſeemed good to me alſo, " having had perfect underſtanding of all things from the very " firſt, to write unto thee in order, moſt excellent Theophilus, " that thou mighteſt know the certainty of thoſe things wherein " thou haſt been inſtructed." The laſt verſe might be more literally rendered, " that thou might know the exact truth of " thoſe doctrines, wherein thou haſt been CATECHIZED." St. Luke's Goſpel therefore, if the writer's own word may be taken about his own work, is an hiſtorical expoſition of the *Catechiſm,* which Theophilus had learned, when he was firſt made a Chriſtian. The two firſt articles, in this hiſtorical expoſition, are the hiſtory of the Baptiſt's birth, and that of Mary's miraculous impregnation. We have much more therefore than the teſtimony of St. Luke, in addition to that of St. Matthew, to the truth of the fact of the Miraculous Conception: we have the teſtimony of St. Luke, that this fact was a part of the earlieſt catechetical inſtruction a part of the catechiſm, no doubt, which St. Paul's converts learnt of the Apoſtle. Let this then be your anſwer, if any man ſhall aſk you a reaſon of this part of your faith; tell him, that you have been learning St. Paul's catechiſm.

C

From

From what hath been said, you will eafily perceive, that the evidence of the fact of our Lord's Miraculous Conception is anfwerable to the great importance of the doctrine; and you will efteem it an objection of little weight, that the modern advocates of the Unitarian tenets cannot otherwife give a colour to their wretched caufe, than by denying the infpiration of the facred hiftorians, that they may feem to themfelves at liberty to reject their teftimony. You will remember, that the doctrines of the Chriftian Revelation were not originally delivered in a fyftem; but interwoven in the hiftory of our Saviour's life. To fay therefore, that the firft preachers were not infpired in the compofition of the narratives, in which their doctrine is conveyed, is nearly the fame thing, as to deny their infpiration in the general. You will perhaps think it incredible, that they, who were affifted by the Divine Spirit when they preached fhould be deferted by that Spirit, when they committed what they had preached to writing. You will think it improbable, that they, who were endowed with the gift of difcerning fpirits, fhould be endowed with no gift of difcerning the truth of facts. You will recollect one inftance upon record, in which St. Peter detected a falfehood by the light of Infpiration: and you will perhaps be inclined to think, that it could be of no lefs importance to the Church, that the Apoftles and Evangelifts fhould be enabled to detect falfehoods in the hiftory of our Saviour's life; than that St. Peter fhould be enabled to detect Ananias's lie about the fale of his eftate. You will think it unlikely that they who were ledde by the Spirit into all truth, fhould be permitted to lead the whole Church for many ages into error: that they fhould be permitted to leave behind them, as authentic

memoirs of their Mafter's life, narratives compiled with little
judgement or felection from the ftories of the day, from facts
and fictions in promifcuous circulation. The credulity, which
fwallows thefe contradictions, while it ftrains at myfteries, is
not the faith which will remove mountains. The Ebionites of
antiquity, little as they were famed for penetration and dif-
cernment, managed however the affairs of the fect with more
difcretion than our modern Unitarians. They queftioned not
the infpiration of the books which they received; but they received only one book, a fpurious copy of St. Matthew's Gofpel,
curtailed of the two firft chapters. You will think it no in-
confiderable confirmation of the doctrine in queftion; that the
fect which firft denied it, to palliate their infidelity, found it
neceffary to reject three of the Gofpels, and to mutilate the
fourth.

Not in words therefore and in form, but with hearts full of
faith and gratitude, you will join in the folemn fervice of the
day, and return thanks to God " who gave his only begotten
" Son to take our nature upon him, and, as at this time, to be
" born of a pure Virgin " You will always remember that it is
the great ufe of a found faith, that it furnifhes the moft effec-
tual motives to a good life. You will therefore not reft in the
merit of a fpeculative faith. You will make it your conftant
endeavour that your lives may adorn your profeffion——that
" your light may fo fhine before men, that they, feeing your
' good works, may glorify your Father which is in heaven "

F I N I S.

Lightning Source UK Ltd.
Milton Keynes UK
UKHW030038260221
379395UK00008B/1729